Spiros Hadjidjanos
Network Time

1 The concept of the "wireless subject" is described at length in Adrian Mackenzie's *Wirelessness: radical empiricism in network cultures* (Cambridge: MIT Press, 2010).

2 Mackenzie, *Wirelessness*, 95.

Elvia Wilk

Nodes and networks

In 1959, the American engineer Paul Baran was charged by the RAND Corporation with the task of designing a telecommunications network resilient enough to survive a nuclear attack. A year later Baran published his proposed solution: a network of distributed nodes without a centralized core. He argued that a distributed network would be indestructible because the connections between its nodes were redundant; multiple connections safeguard a system from total destruction if individual nodes are damaged. A decade later, Baran's distributed relay node architecture formed the conceptual framework for the first system of inter-networked computers, which would become the basis for today's decentralized wireless internet.

In the various iterations of his installation *Network Time,* Spiros Hadjidjanos charts the topology of our contemporary wireless terrain – the virtual/physical surface of wireless networks through which we communicate – uncovering the interlocking system of nodes and redundant connections upon which this intangible landscape is constructed. As we simultaneously navigate and construct this space we ourselves become nodes, receivers and transmitters of data contributing to the redundancy and therefore the imperviousness of the system. We become "wireless subjects," in the words of Adrian Mackenzie. [1]

In many of his installations, videos, sculptures and photographic prints, Hadjidjanos maps and visualizes the territories of networked technology. Yet in particular his iterative installation *Network Time* elucidates how the contemporary condition of "wirelessness" is not only a set of spatial but also temporal relations. Remote communication refers not only to long distances but to remote times; a phone call or an email occurs at once in two – or three, or potentially infinite – time zones. Transmitter and receiver are connected, a spatio-temporal link between nodes is formed, and time folds between the points.

Network Time hones in on the wireless router: the peculiar object that forges and maintains but most importantly *represents* the condition of wirelessness. In the installation a series of active routers are lined up on the floor of a darkened exhibition space, each with a long fiber-optic cable extending from the LED light embedded in its surface. Viewers of the installation are free to log on to the wireless networks belonging to each of the routers, and a user's activity within a given network affects the speed and syncopation of light as information is sent and received. With the cables magnifying and elongating the patterns of flickering light, an abstract information-signal is manifested as a spatio-temporal relationship. Made linear, the signal is made literal, dramatizing the link between nodes.

The router is an unusual object of study. Crucial yet unremarkable, "wireless devices are sometimes infrastructures and sometimes highly intimate possessions," in the words of Mackenzie.[2] As with most types of banal infrastructure, we notice its presence only when it fails. Then, with an exasperated sigh, we crouch down to unplug and replug some wires until the lights start blinking in an assuring manner again.

3 Ibid., 7.

4 Adrian Mackenzie, *Transductions: bodies and machines at speed* (London: Continuum, 2010), 70–17.

5 Levi R. Bryant, *The Democracy of Objects* (Michigan: Open Humanities Press, 2011), 31, 71, 120, 153.

6 Mackenzie, *Transductions*, 14.

Despite the boundless freedom of the infinite network we conceptualize, it is this constant sensation of "weak connections, the residual weight of wires, and barely felt interference" that Mackenzie locates at the heart of wirelessness.[3] Wirelessness is a state of being, of entanglement in a wired network even when the wires are gone.

To manifest or visualize the router's signal is to unfold the synapse of wireless information exchange. Mackenzie describes two ways that technologies fold time: "One technology, a car, consists of technology from across millennia, oldest to newest, and therefore time within it folds." Second, a technology links "two points in a network previously separated by distance or display [and] causes time within the collective to fold."[4] Like the car, or the hammer, or the microchip, the router is a vertical folding of the history of its own development as a tool and a horizontal folding of simultaneous nodes in a network. The artwork *Network Time* elucidates those folds by unfolding them.

News of a difference

In another iteration of *Network Time* titled *Concentric Networked Projections,* Hadjidjanos translates the routers' LEDs into projections rather than extending them with fiber-optic cables. Three routers hang behind one another from the ceiling, projecting glowing-green circles onto the facing wall; the diameter of each circle is scaled according to its respective distance from the projection surface. The circular projections flicker according to wireless activity by gallery-goers logged into each network. This manifestation of the network, while relying on a similar premise, affords an entirely different spatial understanding of the network beyond the linearity of wires. Rather than a line connecting two distinct points – or extending from the router off in one singular direction to infinity – the circular projections manifest the networks as dimensional patches or fields.

In this case, the hanging routers and their projections wobble slightly according to air disturbance in the space, visually enacting the way that signals interfere with each other just as objects do when they come into contact. Their slightly-perceptible turbulence indicates the mesh of object relations they inhabit, evoking Levi Bryant's term "perturbation," with which he describes the way objects and relations affect each other by minutely altering each other's system states through various types of disturbance.[5] Routers perturb each other. They do not communicate directly with humans; they communicate with other objects. If, as Mackenzie writes, "an object is only technical if it occurs in relation with other objects," then the router is only technical.[6]

But technical objects are made by humans for human means. The lights are, ostensibly, there to indicate something to the user, specifically that data packets are being successfully transmitted from one device to another. Each brand of router has its idiosyncrasies (red light might indicate power failure; amber might indicate slow connection speed) but in any case the lights are the sole signals that networked activity is occurring – in fact the only indication that a network exists. We rest assured that information is moving in space.

7 Bryant, *The Democracy of Objects*, 156.
8 Ibid., 157.
9 Mackenzie, *Transductions*, 22.
10 From Hadjidjanos's conversation with Harman in this book.

The strange thing about the blinking light is precisely our confidence in it, our belief that it conveys meaning. In truth the light tells us only that *something* is happening. Semiotically speaking, the little LED is a floating signifier. The router's functionality is so estranged from the *expression* of its functionality that it requires a certain cognitive leap to assume there is any content to the message. The router is barely an interface; information is represented to the human user, but the content of the message is inaccessible without a third-party device. To test the validity of a connection one must refer to a laptop or phone. The content of the information conveyed is the fact that information is being transmitted.

Bryant writes, "information is not a property of a substance, but rather an event that befalls or happens to a substance and which selects a system state."[7] According to him, information is essentially "news of a difference," news that a new element has been added to the system and that therefore the structure of the system has changed. If we adhere to this logic, the mere indication of "news" from the blinking light of the router is enough to constitute information itself.

Bryant also makes a distinction between new and repeated information: he writes that repeated information may not convey news, but it still carries meaning. In his words, "A piece of information that is repeated is no longer information. It retains its meaning in repetition but loses its value as information."[8] Much of the pinging of data packets that a router does is a constant repetition of the same test; it's simply checking that the connection is intact. This is an entirely redundant behavior that sends no news but nevertheless carries great meaning. With Baran's model of a distributed network in mind, the meaning is that the system is intact.

To the wireless subject, information is a function of speed. The faster the blinking, supposedly, the more information is moving and the more powerful the network is. The router in Hadjidjanos's installation is foremost a timekeeper; it expresses how time is produced by technology. Mackenzie writes, "There is no pure, non-technical apprehension of speed, nor any non-technical aspect to time."[9] It's as impossible to conceive of time as a construct as it is to conceive of time without use of a construct.

To manifest a relation as object

Within the tensile mesh of a distributed network, it becomes possible to conceive of the relations between fixed entities themselves as objects. Graham Harman's object-oriented philosophy, for instance, is built on the premise that connections – or connectivity itself – is an object or series of objects on par with nodes. For Harman, "All that something needs to count as an object...is that it cannot be exhaustively reduced either to its internal components or to its outward effects."[10]

Hadjidjanos' work, in line with such realist philosophies, treats relations as such; through multiple points of entry, he asks what it could mean to manifest a "relation as object." *Network Time* is a manifestation of the information-event. More accurately, it is a manifestation of the temporal system that networked wireless devices both engender and rely upon. But what is "manifestation" and what is its use?

11 Mackenzie, *Wirelessness*, 7.

12 In an art context, "wirelessness" could present a welcome alternative for the lauded/reviled term "post-internet." The meaning of "post-internet art" is regularly contested, but it generally refers to work that is not medium-specific to online platforms but that is influenced by the condition of living within a networked society. In other words, post-internet artists do not necessarily make internet art; they make art within a field afforded by and predicated on the possibility of doing so. "Wireless art" operates similarly but without the jarring pre/post setup, a chronology that denies the simultaneity of a network.

13 *Local Manifestations* was the title of a 2013 exhibition by Hadjidjanos at Future Gallery in Berlin.

Whether or not one buys into an object-oriented framework, such an ontology proves a useful way to consider the role of the art object as a *manifestation* as distinct from *materialization*. If materiality is not what distinguishes objects from relations, to try and materialize a relation into a sculpture would be a moot effort. To freeze a dynamic system into a tangible image or object would amount to little more than illustration of one aspect of the system, a synecdoche. Relations can't be spatially or temporally isolated via materialization of their parts. As Anna Munster and Geert Lovink put it, "Theorising networks...must struggle with the abstraction of dispersed elements – elements that cannot be captured into one image. The very notion of a network is in conflict with the desire to gain an overview.'" [11]

Materialization is the attempt to represent a dynamic system via reproduction of one part – regardless of whether the reproduction itself is *material* in the "old-fashioned" sense. Manifestation is an attempt to become part of a system. Both efforts necessarily alter whatever set of relations they react to; but the latter is an iterative process dependent upon time and place. When applied in analysis of an artwork, the distinction drawn here between the two 'M's does not correlate to a distinction between "passive" and "active" art; it does not dichotomize painting and performance, or set up a hierarchy between action and intervention. If objecthood is not about being a rock or a stick, then these typical dichotomies are unhelpful tools for analyzing the way an artwork operates, particularly an artwork whose medium and subject is that of networked technology.[12]

Within the context of *Network Time,* the router – or, more specifically, its blinking light – represents wirelessness. The installation as a whole entity within an exhibition space is a manifestation of wirelessness. Upon entering the space, a visitor is likewise manifested as a wireless subject.

While manifestation in one "local" area network might seem to imply the existence of a "global" one, wirelessness is precisely the condition that makes such a divide irrelevant, or impossible. It is this collapse that *Network Time* responds to. The local is not contrasted here with the global. It does not imply an opposition between the singular and fixed or the multiple and connective, but rather contextualizes each installation of the work as one object-relation within a theoretically infinite set of iterations. The multiplicity, or redundancy of its outward relations is what is responsible for the integrity of its inner relationships. The installation is not "reducible either to its internal components or to its outward effects."

As with a wireless network, a local manifestation (or Local Area Network) is predicated upon system access.[13] You have to know the network name and password to log on. Or, to take a step back, you have to have access to a power grid and broadband connection. A local manifestation depends on endless concentric global circuits of access; a router is impotent without a socket. *Network Time* manifests the concept of access on varying levels: in reference to the literal acts of "plugging in" and "logging on," but also according to the metaphysics of what it means to access an object as such.

10

The Network Time installation does not carry an implicit revelatory agenda; it does not intend to "reveal" an invisible system nor convey 29a moral commentary on the sinister nature of invisibility. Its goal is to locally manifest a network and therefore to demonstrate how manifestation and access are one and the same. For a network is composed of access points; each node is simply a point of access. To access the network is to create the network.

1 Graham Harman, *Towards Speculative Realism*, (Winchester, UK & Washington, USA: Zero Books, 2010), 93.

2 Alexander Galloway, "The Poverty of Philosophy: Realism and Post-Fordism" in *Critical Inquiry*, Vol. 39, No. 2, Winter 2013.

Spiros Hadjidjanos in conversation with Graham Harman

SH You coined the term "Object-Oriented Philosophy" in 1999. Did Object-Oriented Programming influence your decision? Did you anticipate confusion between the two terms?

GH First I should say that the dating is a bit off the mark, but that's my own mistake. I wrote in *Towards Speculative Realism*[1] that the term was first used in my September 1999 lecture at Brunel University under the title "Object-Oriented Philosophy," which is now one of the chapters of that book. Then someone pointed out that I had already used the phrase in my dissertation. That led me to scour my hard drive, and then I discovered the term in my notes as early as 1997.

The term was stolen directly from computer science, of course – but only the term. I was not inspired by any of the detailed features of Object-Oriented Programming, about which I know relatively little. I didn't anticipate the confusion to which you refer, because I think it is quite normal and useful to borrow metaphors from other fields. The term "broadcasting," for instance, originally came from agriculture, but I doubt anyone was confused when it took on a new meaning for mass media purposes.

Many of the confusions we're now seeing with the phrase "object-oriented" are really quite inexcusable, and in some cases are deliberately fabricated for polemical purposes. A shining example would be Alexander Galloway's disingenuous claim that since Object-Oriented Programming is used by evil global corporations, then Object-Oriented Philosophy is somehow complicit in corporate exploitation.[2] There is a "homology" between the two, he says. In layman's terms, "homology" means that there is a verbal resemblance. The reason he didn't just say "verbal resemblance" is because then the weakness of the argument would be clear even to children. It's a bit like saying that the Planters Peanuts logo has a disturbing "homology" with old Prussian expansionism given that monocles are present in both cases. Galloway is smart enough to make a more serious criticism; we could only benefit from it.

Capitalist complicity is also a strange charge to make against a philosophy that has swept into prominence from the margins – community colleges, the developing world, blogs, and small independent presses – unlike many of its critics, who are positioned in well-funded elite establishment institutions.

SH To speak about objects, you have written that objects are "an intermediate being found neither in subatomic physics nor in human psychology, but in a permanent autonomous zone where objects are simply themselves." Does this zone have spatial quality? You have also written that

3 Graham Harman, *The Third Table*, (Ostfildern: Hatje Cantz Verlag, 2012), 10.
4 Graham Harman, "On Vicarious Causation" in *Collapse* Vol. II, (Falmouth: Urbanomic, March 2007), 194.

these objects can be verified in no way at all, whether by science or by tangible effects in human sphere.[3]

GH — This zone is not spatial. For me, "space" is neither a container (as per Newton and Clarke) nor a a system of relations (as per Leibniz), but the *tension* between relation and non-relation. But not everything is locked in such tension at all times. Objects can also be *dormant,* meaning that they are not currently in relation with anything and might never be. Admittedly, for me all objects are composite, which means that they are generated by relations *between their pieces,* but this does not mean that the objects themselves need to be in relation with anything.

SH — I am particularly interested in spatial arrangements. You have written that to occupy a spatial position is to take up relations[4]. Would you say that 'relations' presuppose that you are spatially defined?

GH — Yes. To be in relations is automatically to be spatial, since to relate means to make partial contact with other entities while simultaneously withdrawing from them. Not all relations are located in what we call physical space. There is a broader sense of space that encompasses all relations, physical or otherwise.

SH — In our short discussion in Berlin you mentioned that every relation is itself an object, something that appears frequently in your texts. How do you think the idea of the *relation as an object* can be manifested? I have been thinking about this for a long time.

GH — It was important to free my concept of objects from the traditional concepts of substance, to which I am indebted, but which have certain obvious flaws. Realist philosophers of substance have tended to prefer natural and/or simple entities over artificial and/or compound ones. In the case of Leibniz, even the *eternity* of objects was taken to be important, something Aristotle had already gotten rid of after the pre-Socratic dogma that the cosmic ultimates must be indestructible.

All that something needs to count as an object, for me, is that it cannot be exhaustively reduced either to its internal components or to its outward effects. And this entails that if two things come genuinely into relation, this relation must itself be an object. If the relation is genuine, that it cannot simply be an aggregate made up of its relata, or an event made up of the effects it has here and now.

An example will be helpful. I was recently married. As anyone knows who has been married, there is a pressing reality to the marriage itself that is not reducible to the two individuals. The marriage itself acts as a separate force affecting the actions of both people. In this sense, "our marriage" is not simply a bulk nickname for me and my wife considered as separate individuals. The marriage is not reducible downward

5 Graham Harman, *Quentin Meillassoux: Philosophy in the making*, (Edinburgh: Edinburgh University Press, 2011), 173.

to two people or to the historic chain of events and documents that causally gave rise to it. It has a reality over and above those elements.

But neither is the marriage reducible to its concrete effects. Outsiders can't understand what it's like, but neither do my wife and I really understand what it's like. The marriage has an unfathomable reality that has new consequences at all times. It is more than a list of everything that has happened to both of us since our wedding day.

In this sense, the marriage is different from the people and documents who compose it, and different from its manifestations so far, and even different from all the manifestations it might someday have or might possibly have had. Thus, the marriage is an object. And the same holds true for any genuine relation. I say *genuine* relation because we can always list an arbitrary aggregate of things together without their having any joint objecthood outside my naming of them at the moment.

SH Interviewing Quentin Meillassoux in your book *Quentin Meillassoux: Philosophy in the Making,* you refer to "surprise" as one of the greatest cognitive tools that humans have.[5] To Claude Shannon, the amount of information conveyed is a measure of "surprise" and is closely related to the chance of an occurrence of a particular event – the less probable an event the more surprising it is. In this sense, the more new information an artwork vis-à-vis the art historical context has, the more surprising it is. Could a direct focus on the creation of "surprising" events constitute a method for innovation?

GH Yes, it could. But I don't relate surprise to probability, and neither does Meillassoux. For Meillassoux, the really surprising events are neither probable nor improbable. As long as we can calculate the probability (or lack thereof) of an event, we are in the realm of the potential. By contrast, the virtual for Meillassoux is the realm of events that cannot be called either probable or improbable, since they partake of Cantor's transfinite realm: the emergence of life from matter, thought from life, and justice from thought by way of the God who does not exist and has never existed but might exist in the future.

In my own case, by contrast, even *probable* events can be made surprising. Obviously, you can make an artistic masterpiece out of entirely probable subject matter. Surprise is not a matter of surprise, but of driving a wedge between objects and their qualities. In everyday life we have a tendency to treat objects as being just what British Empiricism says they are: bundles of qualities. But for me both philosophy and art are about creating rifts between objects and their qualities. There really is something there that's deeper than "bundles." In that sense I am a sworn anti-empiricist, despite the current good press surrounding the term "empiricism" (which perhaps even exceeds the good press of another currently popular term I dislike: "pragmatism").

6 Adrian Johnston, *"Hume's Revenge: À Dieu, Meillassoux?"* in *The Speculative Turn: Continental Materialism and Realism*, *L.R. Bryant et al*, ed. (Melbourne: re.press, 2011), 112.

But yes, I think the creation of surprises is the intellectual method par excellence.

SH Let's talk about Speculative Realism. Speculative Realists aim to open the door of a reality that exists outside of human perception which idealism has closed to the world-for-itself. I feel that Speculative Realism is not specific knowledge but an amazing toolbox for creativity. Can you comment on that?

GH Even those who wrongly treat Speculative Realism as just smoke and mirrors, or as the purveying of trivialities already known, eventually have to concede the fact that the term has caught on like wildfire in the humanities. Why has this happened?

We should first consider the chief enemy of all Speculative Realism: "correlationism." This is Meillassoux's term for the basic dogma of all continental and much analytic philosophy that we cannot think of humans without world or the world without humans, but only of a primordial correlation or rapport between the two. Realism was not even taken seriously as an option in continental philosophy until the early twenty-first century. Instead, it was a simple background assumption among continentals that realism vs. anti-realism was a "pseudo-problem" unworthy of serious debate. That view is widespread even today, and not just among crusty old-timers. For example, even as bright and progressive a figure as Adrian Johnston views the Speculative Realist critique of correlationism as a "tempest in a teacup," with realism for Johnston being something to be settled only on the level of detailed scientific practice rather than philosophical speculation itself.[6]

But I doubt that artists will take much inspiration from the notion that realism is a tempest in a teacup. So far they have responded emphatically to Speculative Realism itself rather than to the critiques of it. I think this results, paradoxically, from the fact that art is in some way more realist than the sciences themselves. That is to say, the sciences are happy to replace electrons or neon atoms with lists of discursively expressible properties of these things. In other words, the sciences are under disciplinary pressure to treat objects precisely as bundles of qualities and nothing more. By contrast, the arts are under professional pressure to do exactly the opposite. We know full well that, except in highly contrived special cases, we cannot reduce a painting or sculpture to the atoms of which they are constructed. The reality of an artwork is not the feeble reality of the sciences, too easily translatable into knowledge about that reality.

SH How do you think Speculative Realism could be implemented in the arts?

GH It's already happening. Here you'll need to ask the artists, because I have no desire to legislate how others use my ideas.
But I do think we need to distinguish between different forms of

7 Levi R. Bryant, Graham Harman, Nick Srnicek ed., *The Speculative Turn: Continental Materialism and Realism*, (Melbourne: re.press, 2011) 21.

8 Ray Brassier interviewed by Marcin Rychter, "I Am a Nihilist Because I Still Believe in Truth," *Kronos*, accessed August 21, 2014 www.kronos.org.pl/index.php?23151,896.

Speculative Realism. Here I will say frankly that Ray Brassier's sort of Speculative Realism, which takes a more eliminativist, scientistic line, is unlikely to be of much use to the arts at all – despite Robin Mackay's energetic entrepreneurial efforts to claim otherwise. From that direction I see a completely misguided effort to move towards an "art without humans." But this is impossible, and all it can ultimately mean is an art that points towards situations that people find especially ominous: noise, nihilism, screams in the darkness, and other tokens of the purported worthlessness of the human species. The problem with the human-world correlate (a.k.a. "correlationism," our great shared enemy) is not just the *human* side, as if the "world" side were unproblematic. The problem is treating human and world as the two central terms of reality. But that doesn't mean you can take humans out of art, any more than you can take humans out of politics – or out of basketball, for that matter. An "art without humans" is about as meaningful as the call for a "basketball without humans." It's not an anti-correlationist move at all, but simply an old-fashioned scientistic one, lifting inanimate human nature above all else and eliminating humans in favor of it. I find this to be the *least* promising strand of Speculative Realism.

So let's admit that it's not so much "Speculative Realism" that is influencing the arts as Object-Oriented Philosophy. The reason artists like Object-Oriented Philosophy is because it actually respects artists! After 400 years of science worship and mathematics worship in philosophy, Object Oriented Ontology treats art as something of *cognitive* value, and not simply as a mood stimulant or a vehicle for the expression of one's own psychological, ontological, or scientific prejudices.

SH Referring to the power of a "brand," you wrote that if the decision were yours alone, a Speculative Realist logo would be designed for projection on PowerPoint screens.[7] How do you imagine this logo? Would it share elements with the 2007 Speculative Realism workshop poster at Goldsmiths?

GH I am not literally interested in creating a logo, and have taken no steps towards doing so. The point of those remarks was to express my frustration with the way that others in the group were trying to distance themselves from the name "Speculative Realism."

The history is as follows. Ray Brassier, who has now rejected the name "Speculative Realism" in somewhat violent fashion,[8] was nonetheless the originator of the group and of the name itself. His point was a good one: there's strength in numbers; we all have something in common, yet we are laboring in obscurity. He and Alberto Toscano arranged the 2007 Goldsmiths workshop, and obviously it proved to be a huge success. Everyone benefited – including those who now disown the name. As I see it, that's not the way the game is played. When you sign up for a club you stick with it, and you don't insist too fiercely on your own unique irreducibility to the rest of the group. That is best done on an

9 **Graham Harman, "The current State of Speculative Realism" in Speculations IV, (New York: Punctum, 2013)**

issue-by-issue basis, not by claiming root incommensurability between oneself and everyone else.

Brassier's whole concept of Speculative Realism was as nothing else than a "brand," and it succeeded precisely as a brand. It was an easy way to identify a loose group of thinkers who, even now, have some important things in common, and which was simple and catchy enough to be remembered by those who heard it: just like Impressionism, Fauvism, the Pre-Raphaelite Brotherhood, German Idealism, Actor-Network Theory, and other intellectual brands. But in the year 2013 our anti-capitalism has become so pious that we love to accuse each other of using curse words such as "brand" and "speculation." Yet precisely for that reason, the favorite metaphors of capitalism gain a new contrarian force, and hence anyone interested in the craft of writing cannot avoid experimenting with them.

As I've pointed out in a recent article,[9] there's nothing the four original Speculative Realists can do to remove each other's names from their eventual obituaries, so why be so finicky about the term? "Speculative Realism" oversimplified all of us – as all group names do – but also gave us the visibility that, frankly, we had earned.

SH You are posting on your blog almost on daily basis. How does this affect what we read in your books?

GH Blogging can have the same beneficial effects as sports writing, which I did for a time in graduate school. It forces you to keep writing on deadline, and in a punchy and accessible manner. Sports writing is perhaps the best thing that ever happened to me, since it was my first experience of needing to write in large quantities in an invigorating, non-academic way.

I first started blogging in January 2009, and found it exhilarating. But I soon found it exhausting to engage in so many back-and-forth exchanges with commenters, even with the constructive commenters. And as is well known, there is an unusually large amount of low-quality human interaction in the blogosphere as well.

So, things evolved towards the current state of my blog, where it's more of an intellectual snack bar: featuring links, ad-hoc comments, and an occasional meaty post. I can't do what Levi Bryant does and engage in constant lengthy dialogues with people on my blog, because I find it physically and mentally exhausting, and it would severely cut into the productivity of my own writing. It seems to work well for Levi, but I prefer to use the blog for links and off-the-cuff observations, saving my best work for books, articles, and lectures.

1 Adrian Mackenzie, *Wirelessness: radical empiricism in network cultures* (Cambridge: MIT Press, 2010), 193.

2 Ibid., 61.

Spiros Hadjidjanos **in conversation with Adrian Mackenzie**

SH You coined the term "Wirelessness," which is also the title of one of your books. Can you explain how you came up with the term and what it means?

AM I'm not sure I came up with this term. I've seen it used elsewhere since, and I don't know if it pre-dated my use of it. I think it was coined between 2001–2005, when wireless networks were suddenly becoming visible in many different places, ranging from cafes to international development programs. "Wirelessness" refers to the specific material fabric of the contemporary experience of movement and communication.

SH You have called people "wireless subjects." Do these subjects belong to the "Internet of Things," as defined by Bruce Sterling?

AM I guess people as wireless subjects do belong to the Internet of Things in some ways, but that very concept has changed so much it's hard to say. It seems that Bruce Sterling's vision of traceable, verifiable and perhaps more democratic communication does not encompass many of the subsequent developments in network data flows. Wireless networks and wirelessness is so much more banal – perhaps even contaminated – than the Internet of Things seemed to be.

SH In *Wirelessness* you create an association between William James' philosophy of Radical Empiricism and your concept of Wireless Networks. What was the origin of relating these two concepts?

AM It might seem a strange choice since James' work has been largely understood as pragmatic. But James' work in general re-defines experience in terms of movements, paths, and various forms of conjunctive relation. This seemed to me a potentially rich and evocative way of thinking about what was and is still happening as communication is reorganised.

SH You summarized James's Radical Empiricism by writing that it suspends distinctions such as subject versus object, represented versus representation, and thinking versus thing[1], and that for James relations exist as much as things.[2] To me this system suggests a flat ontology similar to that found in Object-Oriented Philosophy.

AM To be honest, I didn't know about Object-Oriented Philosophy at the time. Since then I have read some. For me, it was much more immediately the work of Isabelle Stengers, Brian Massumi and to a certain extent Bruno Latour that first steered me toward James. I can see why the approach I took might seem like flat ontology. Certainly there is flattening

3 Ibid., 58.

4 Adrian Mackenzie, Transductions: bodies and machines at speed (London: Continuum, 2010), 3.

5 Ibid., 92.

or cross-linking of some of standard dualisms (thinking vs. thing; living vs. non-living, subject-object etc.), but the shifting density and mutable envelope of experience in James does not feel so flat to me. Rather, for me, it highlights variations, fluctuations, senses of connectedness and disconnection in a much more lively way.

SH Are there any other philosophical systems that you find pertinent to Wireless Networks?

AM I'm not keen on philosophical systems. I think it would be interesting to work more with Maurizio Lazzarato's "Video Philosophy" or perhaps Sloterdijk's "atmospheres" in relation to wireless signal processing.

SH When discussing urban infrastructure, you wrote that the idea of the Wireless City terminates in a movement, not in a place.[3] Can you elaborate on that?

AM Yes, it's a slightly cryptic thing to say. I was referring to James' notion of experience. In many ways, I see radical empiricism and its account of experience as full as conjunctions as a philosophy of urbanism. In that sense, any endpoint is a provisional, and will lead to new departures.

SH Working with the physical and conceptual properties of networks, I'm interested to know where you believe physical network architecture ends and where virtual network architecture begins. Is this delineation variable or is it possible to separate the virtual and physical aspect of technological networks?

AM I'm always nervous around the virtual. What sense of the virtual are we talking about? And from where are we talking about it? I guess my method of working with things, techniques and larger assemblies like network is to try to find the places where people move between different layers or levels. In these places, the line between the physical and anything else is in question. These places might be control rooms, they might be certain technical interfaces, they might be everyday, down-to-earth hacks or work-arounds, or they might an art installation. I particularly like and look for loopy places, where the levels are confused with each other. For instance, in relation to virtuality, I'd be tempted to study "virtualization" practices in the Cloud.

SH In your book *Transductions* you wrote, "the problem of thinking about technology is also a problem of thinking about time."[4] With devices like the Google Glass, in the near future we will be able to measure the amount and the quality of information we receive in a more precise way. What could this data tell us about our subjective reality and sense of temporality? Drawing on your interest in Heidegger's insistence that "clocks provide no insight

28

into time"[5], do you think that data analysis could provide insight into a kind of time that clocks cannot tell? Or, to put it naively: days full of new information feel very short whereas days of low activity are long and boring. Do you see a relation between information and our sense of time in the context of information theory?

AM Will we be able to measure time, or will someone else? At the moment, there is little sign that the flows of subjectivity-data we generate are in any way given back to us. They are stored and worked on elsewhere. Would Google Glass change that? Google doesn't have a good track record on sharing its data, even though it provides abundant search results and other services. That said, I agree that the data being generated and captured by such devices suggest different ways of thinking about and acting in the world. Maybe the Quantified Self movement has this possibility in mind. Analyzing all the data generated in daily life, however, is not easy. I'm hoping that the predictive models based on this data won't be made totally in the service of selling me stuff or checking whether I pose a security risk to some State. I'm hoping for much more creative, surprising forms of prediction, which might be a contradictory hope.

SH How would you compare a router to clock?

AM This is a provocative question. It would take a lot of work to answer it. Which clock and which router do you have in mind? I'd like to compare specific models!

Both interviews were conducted in Spring 2013
Image on page 41: Concentric Networked Projections
All other images: Network Time

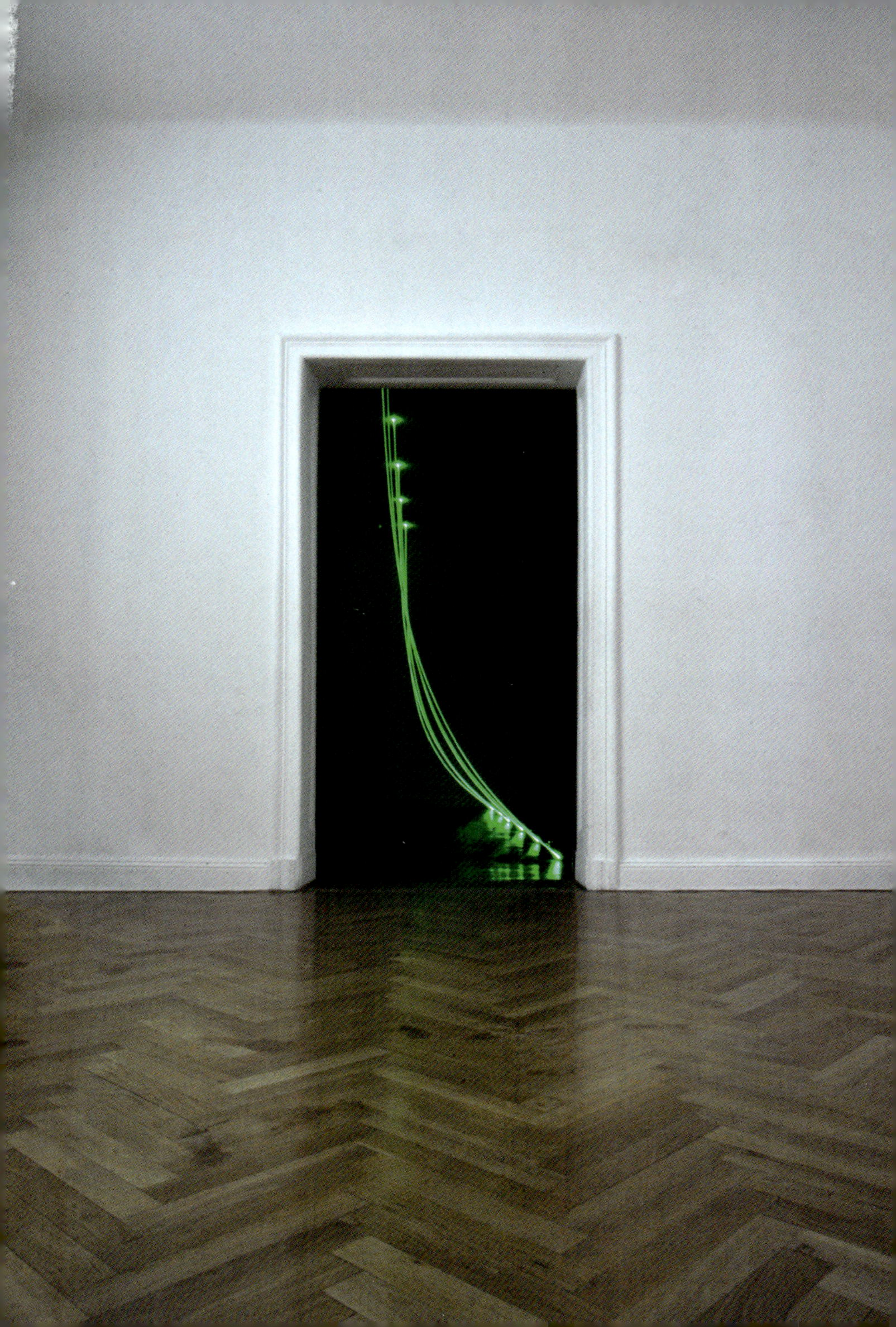

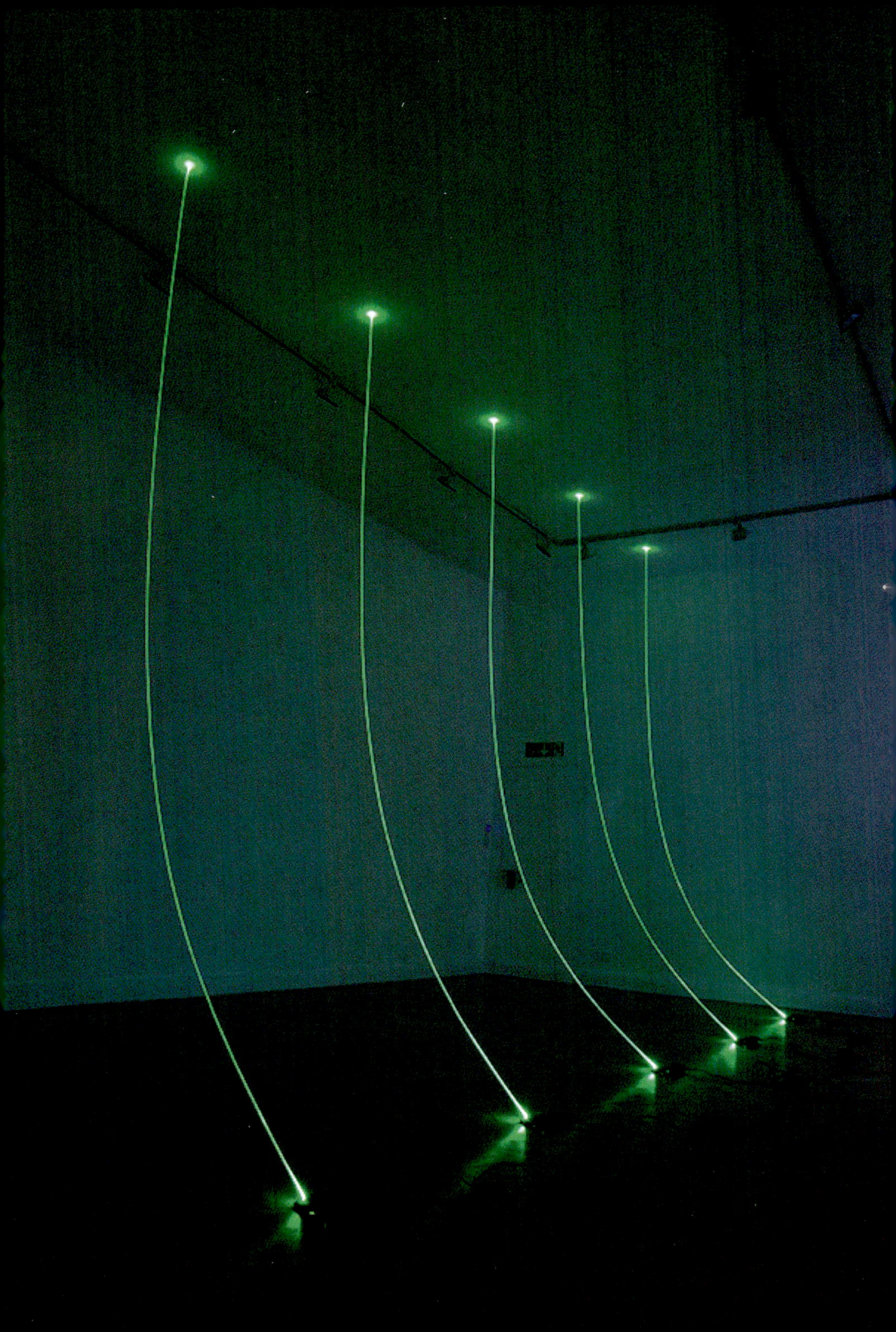

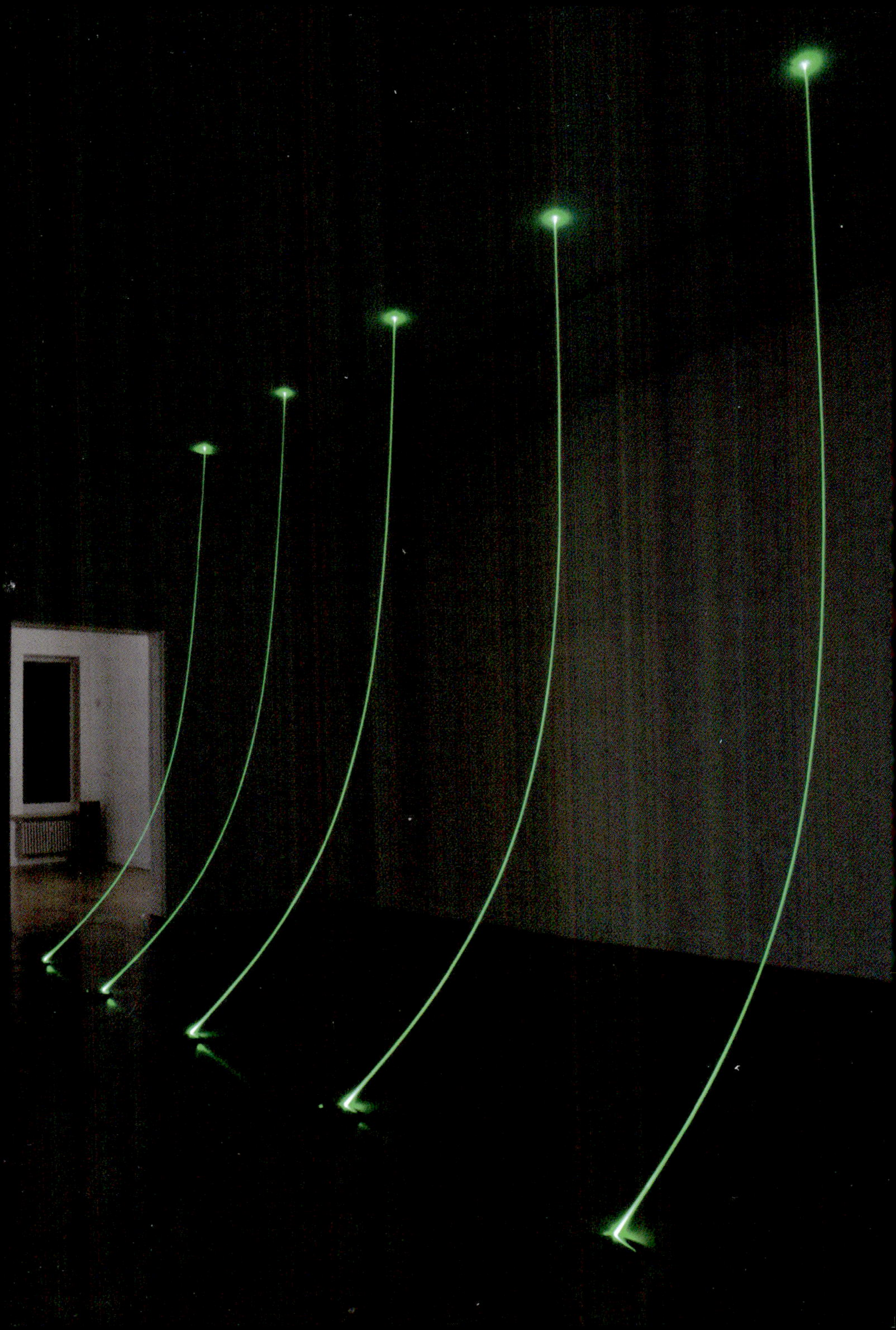

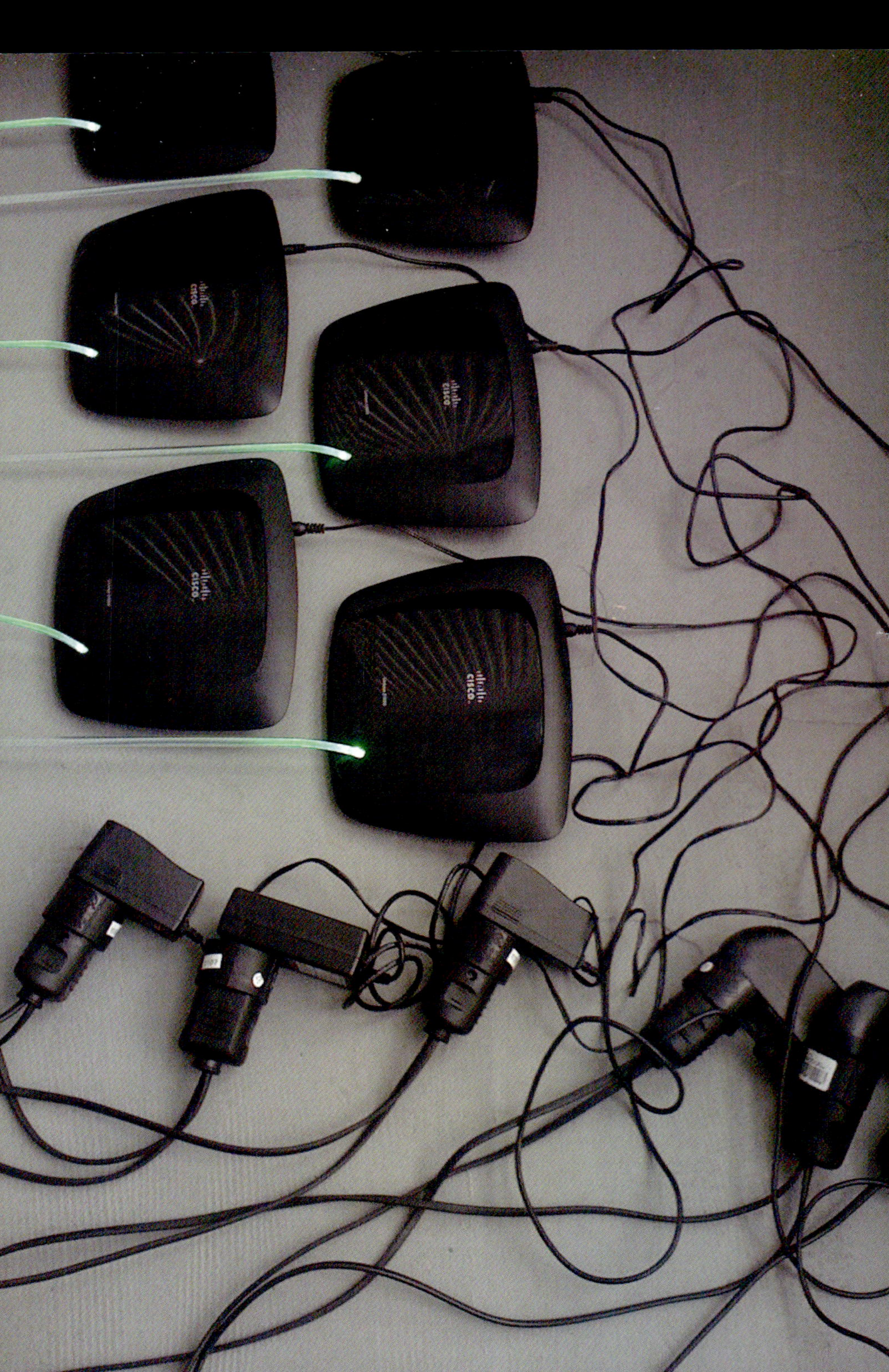
cisco
cisco
cisco
cisco

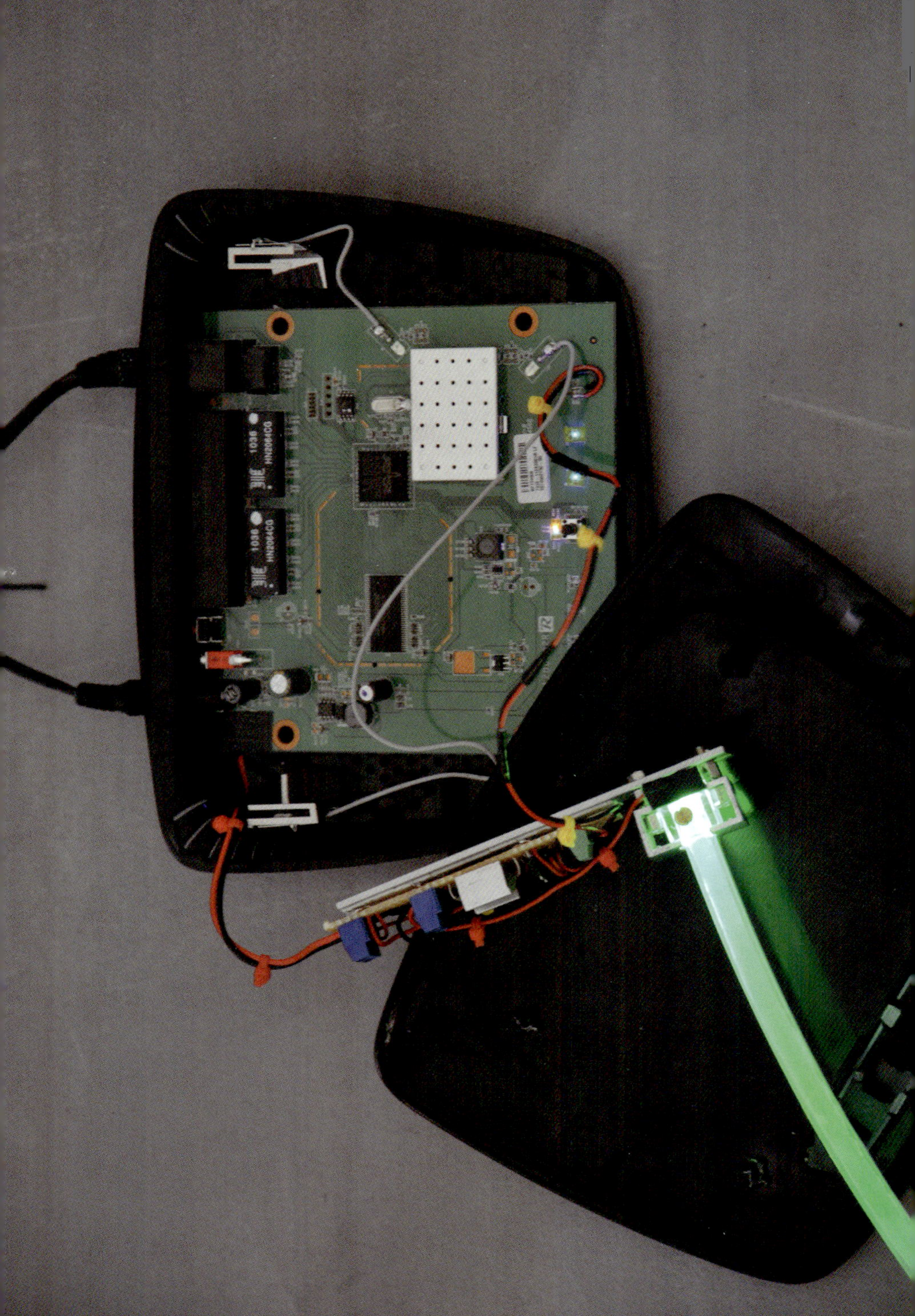

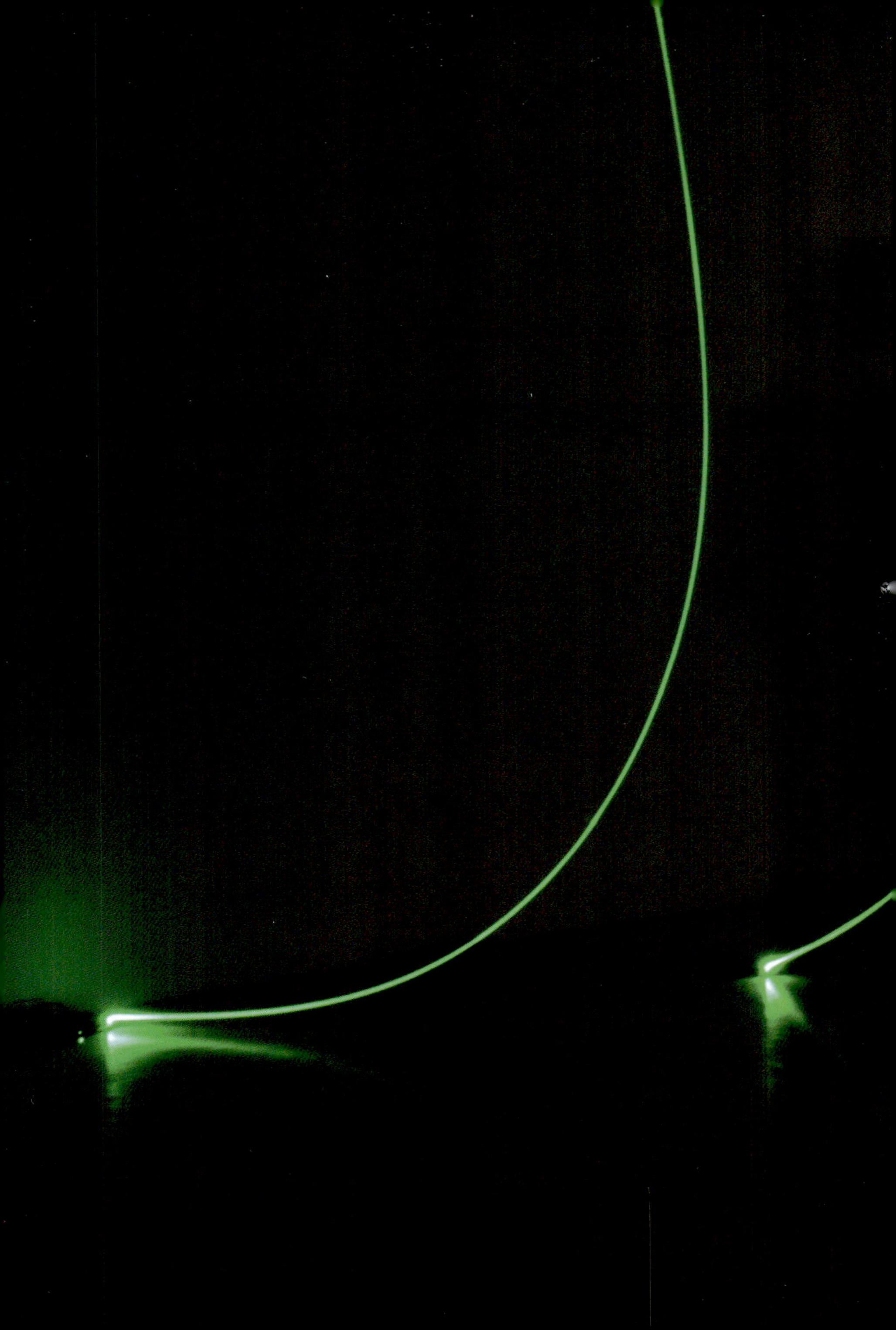

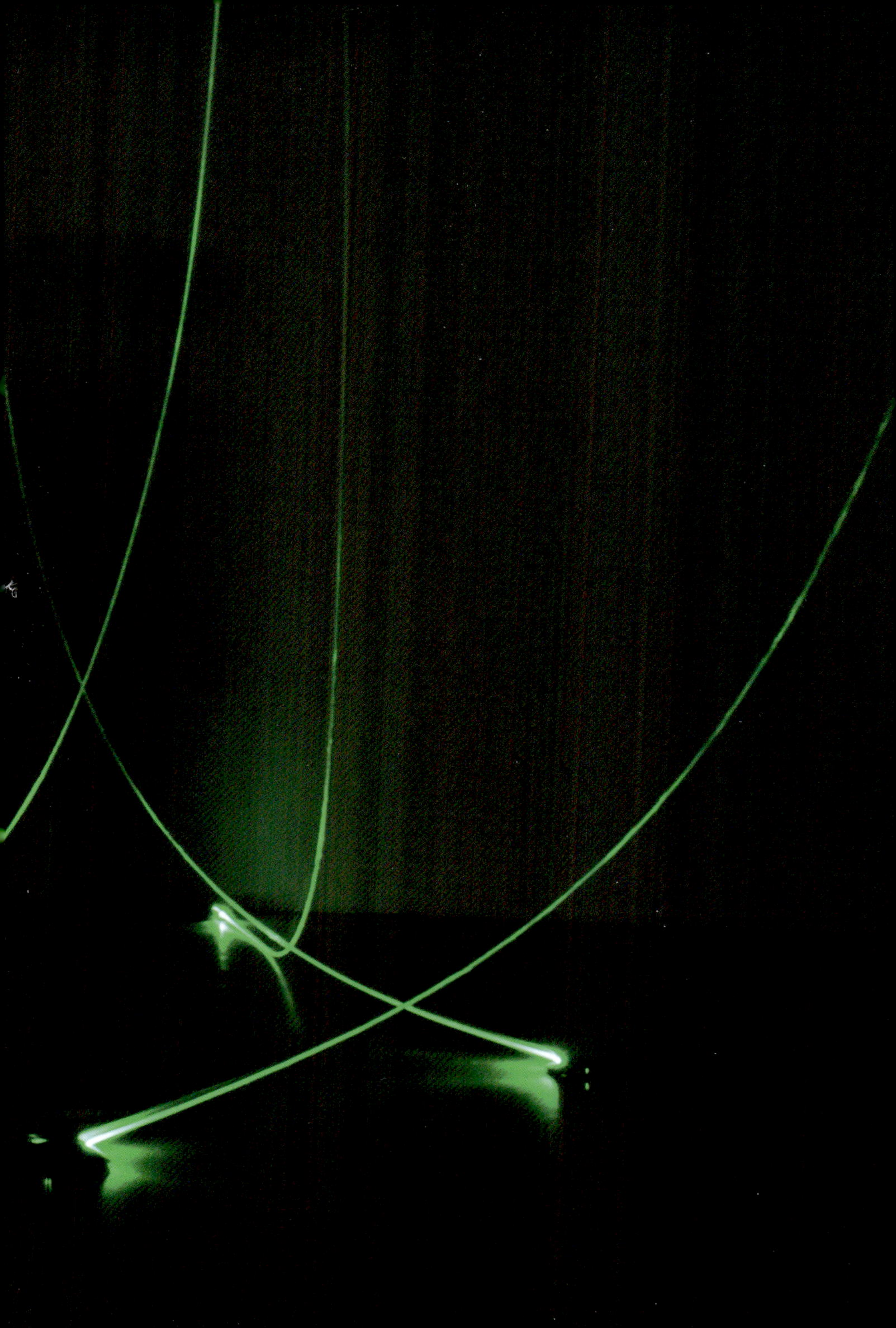

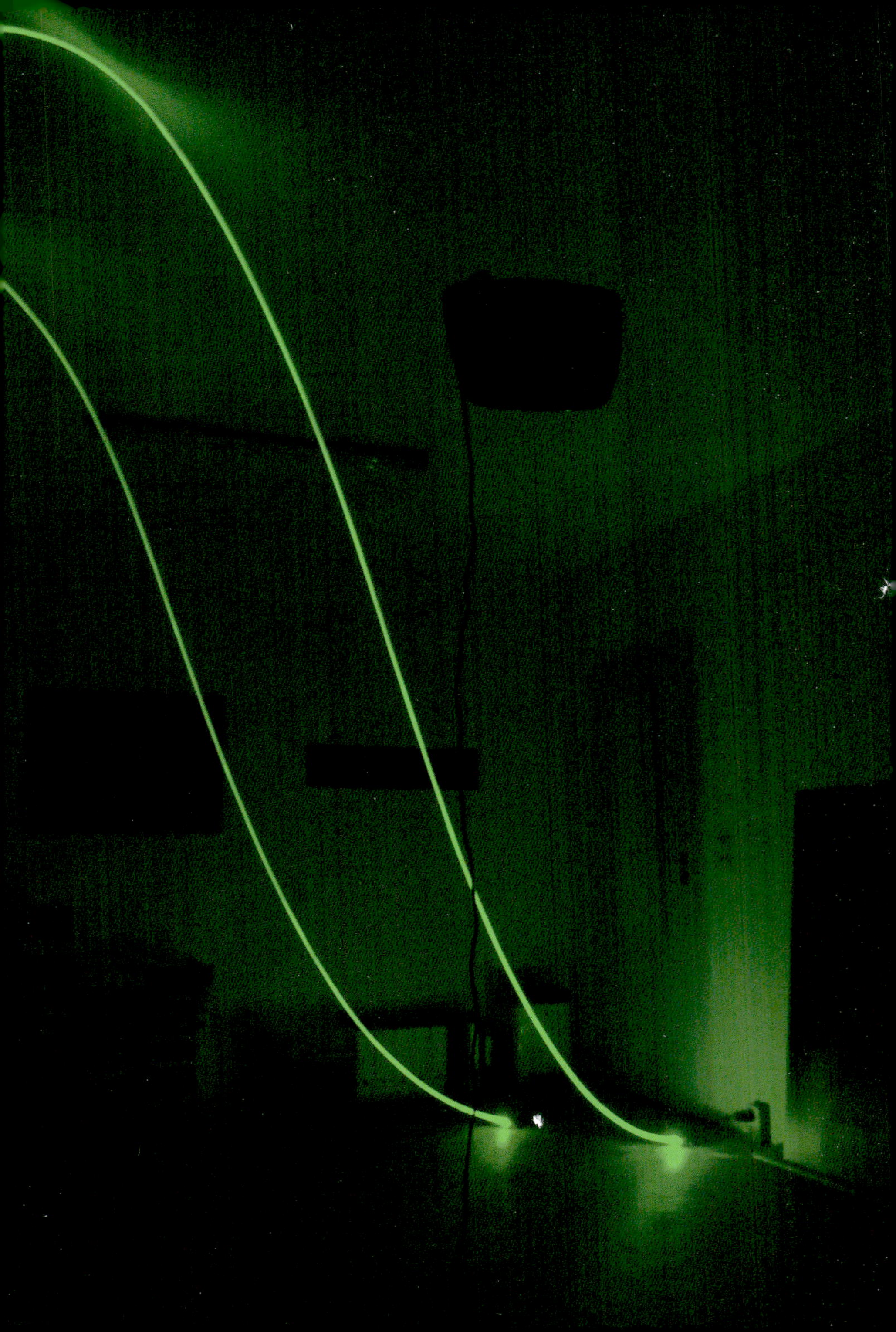

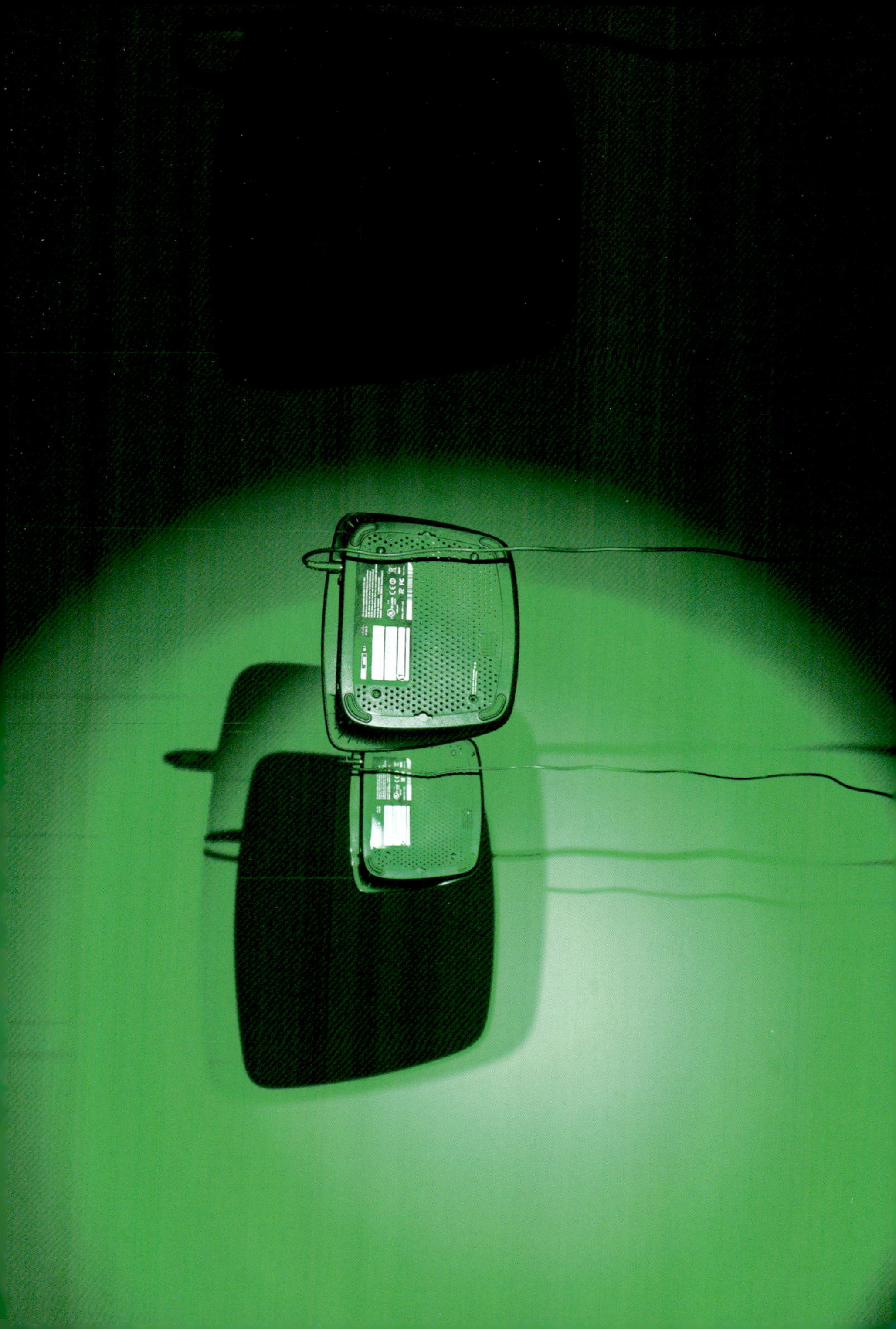

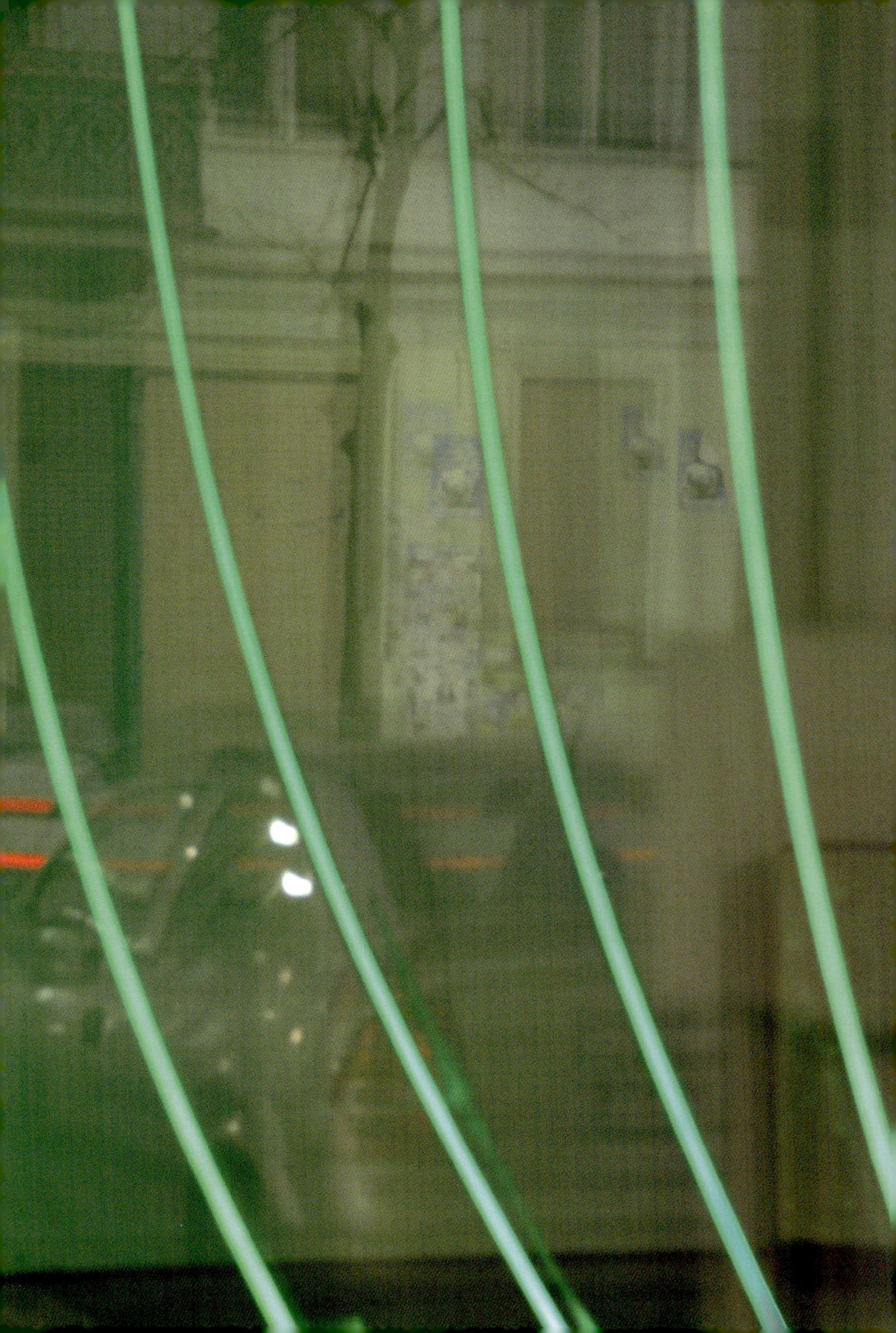

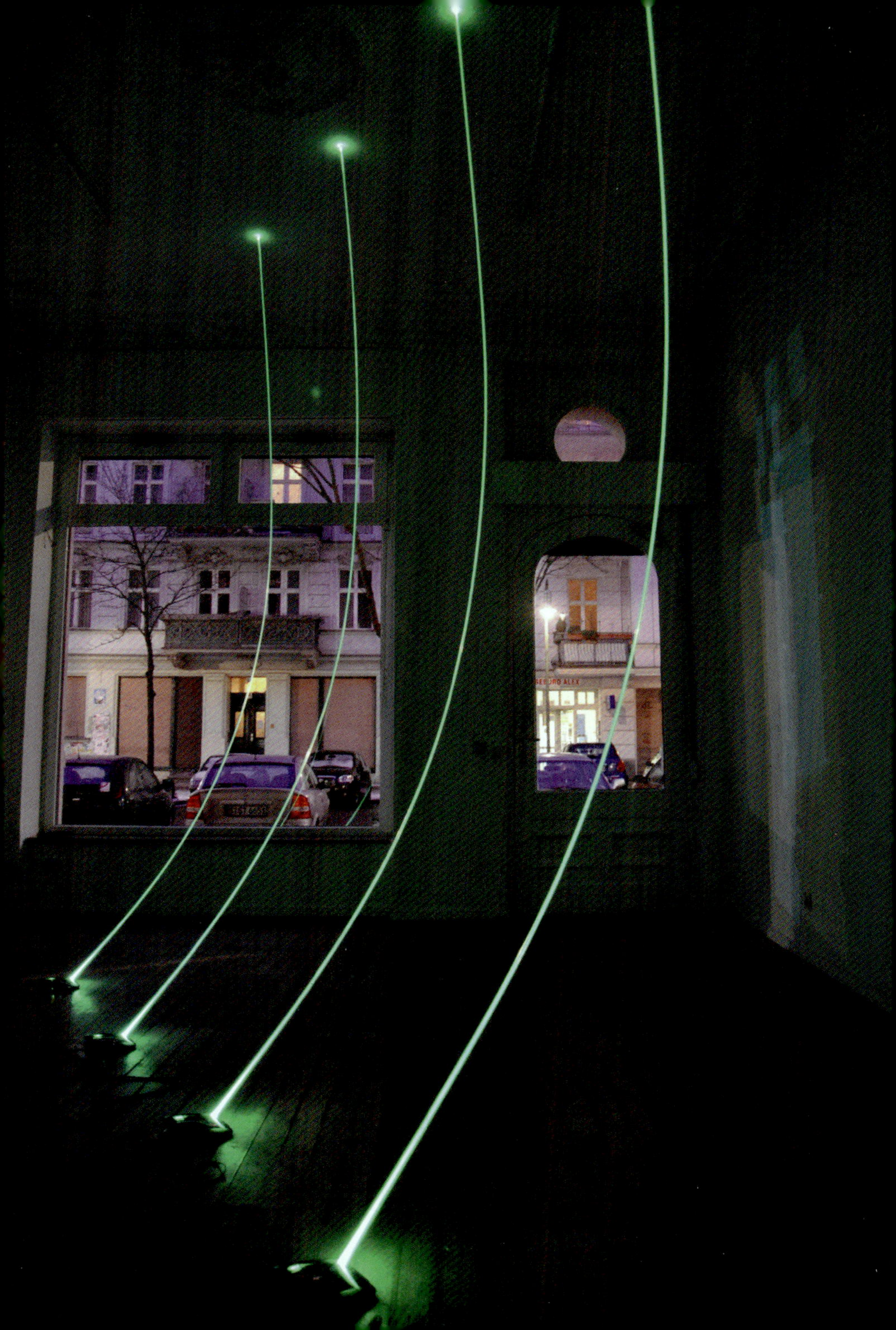

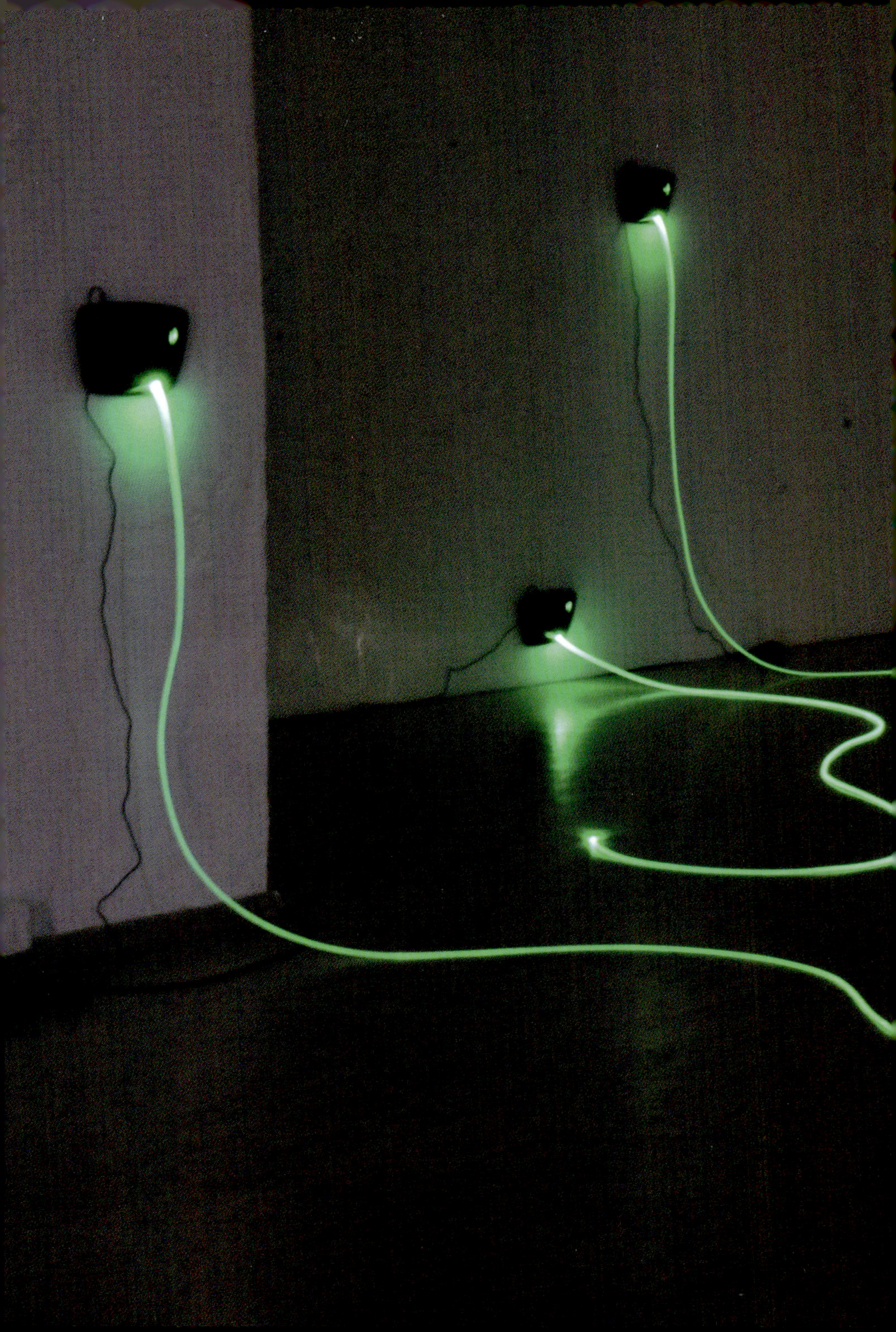

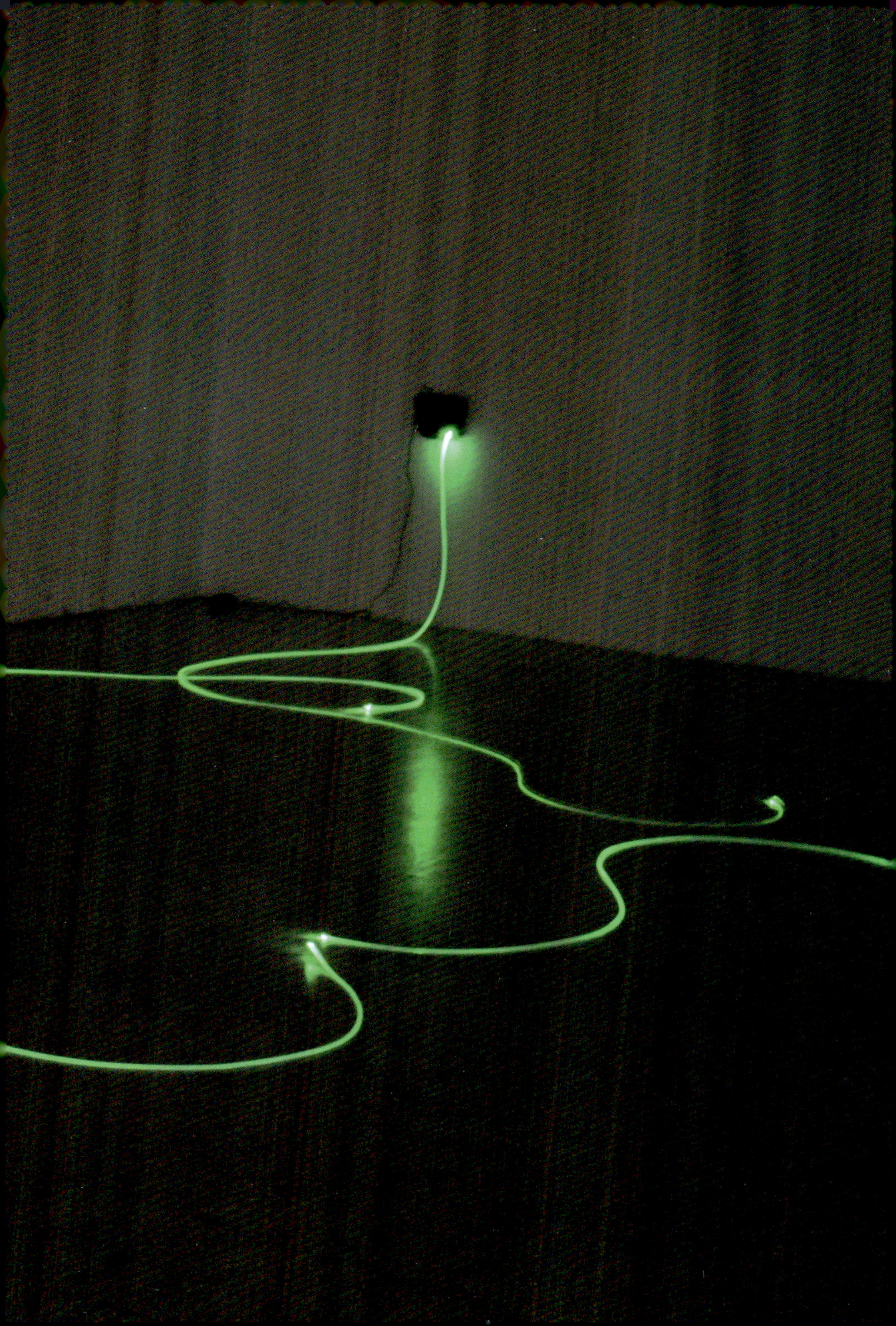

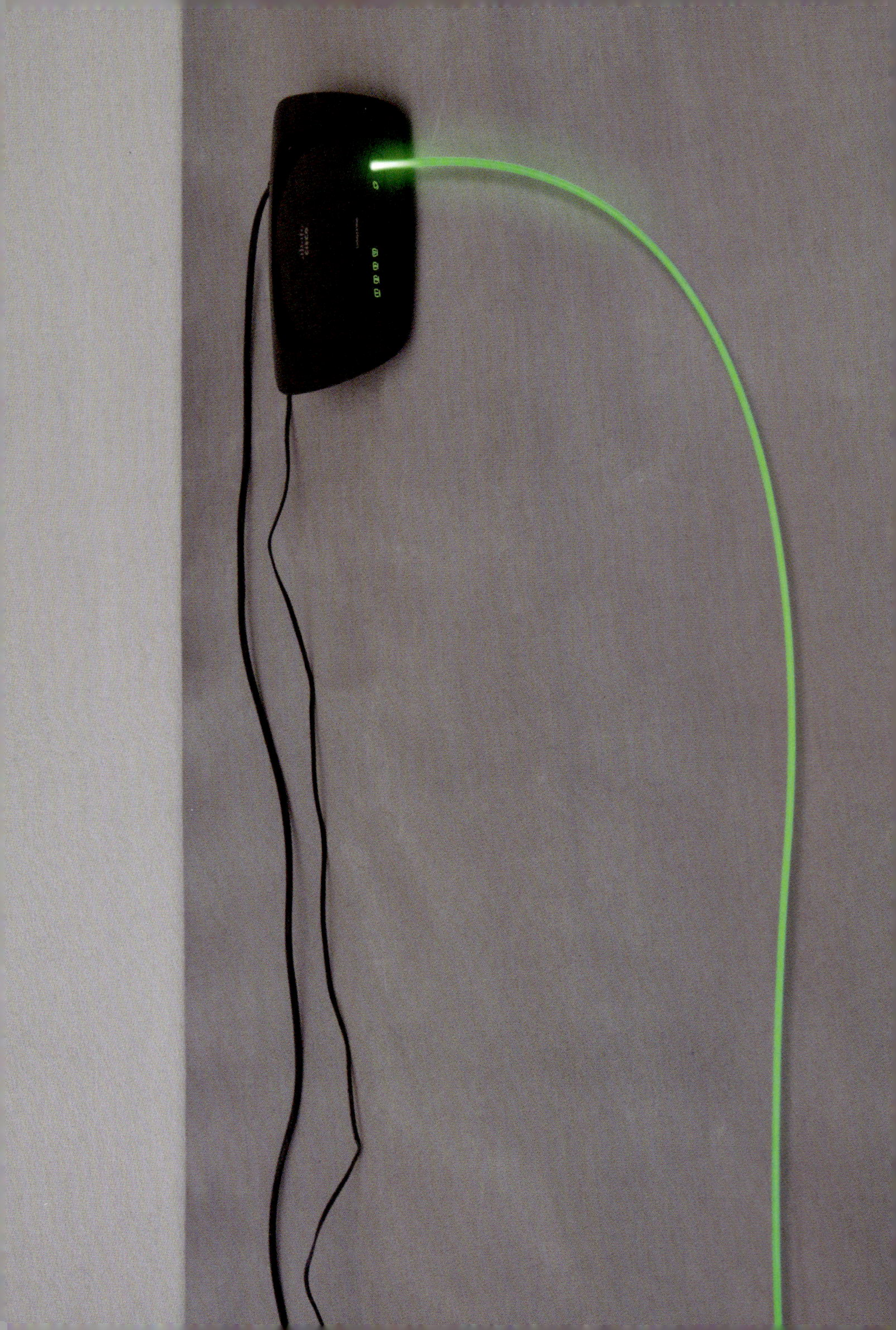

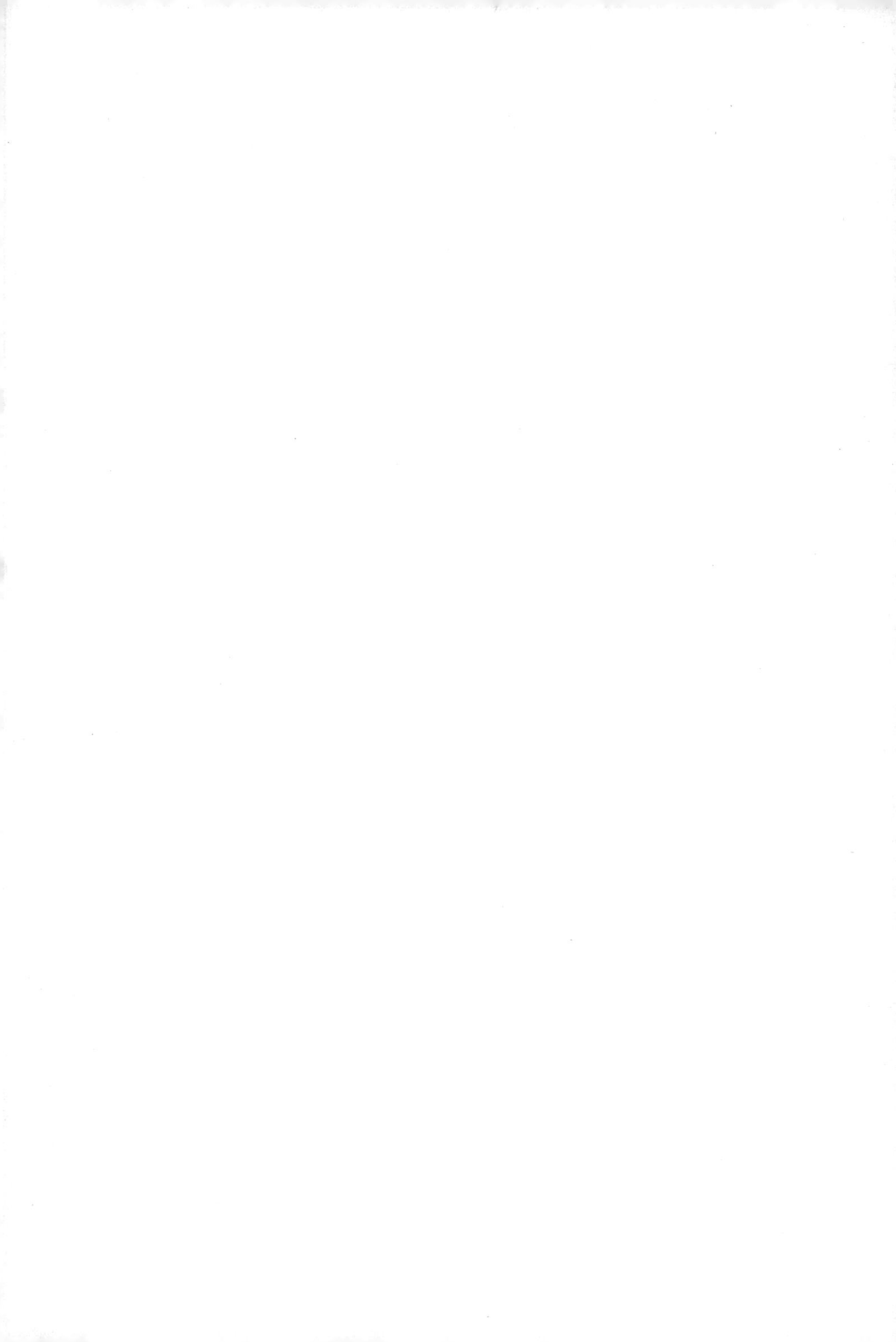

APE#042
Spiros Hadjidjanos, Network Time

ISBN 9789490800253
www.artpapereditions.org
www.spiroshadjidjanos.net
First edition of 300 copies

Graphic design: Studio Jurgen Maelfeyt
Printing: New Goff, Ghent
First print: August 2014